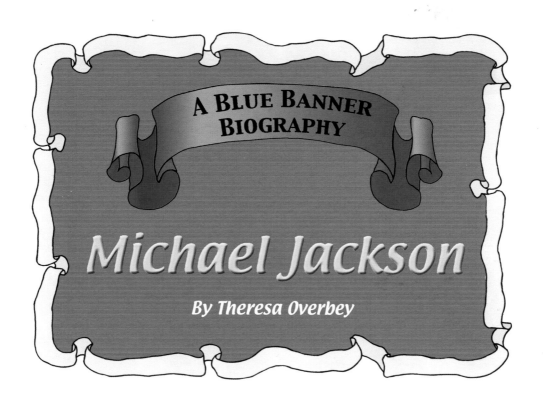

A BLUE BANNER
BIOGRAPHY

Michael Jackson

By Theresa Overbey

Mitchell Lane
PUBLISHERS

P.O. Box 196
Hockessin, Delaware 19707
Visit us on the web: www.mitchelllane.com
Comments? email us: mitchelllane@mitchelllane.com

Mitchell Lane
PUBLISHERS

Printing   2   3   4   5   6   7   8   9

Blue Banner Biographies

Alicia Keys	Allen Iverson	Ashanti
Ashlee Simpson	Ashton Kutcher	Avril Lavigne
Beyoncé	Bow Wow	Britney Spears
Christina Aguilera	Christopher Paul Curtis	Clay Aiken
Condoleezza Rice	Daniel Radcliffe	Derek Jeter
Eminem	Eve	Ja Rule
Jay-Z	Jennifer Lopez	J.K. Rowling
Jodie Foster	Justin Berfield	Kate Hudson
Lance Armstrong	Lindsay Lohan	Mario
Mary-Kate and Ashley Olsen	Melissa Gilbert	**Michael Jackson**
Missy Elliott	Nelly	P. Diddy
Paris Hilton	Queen Latifah	Ritchie Valens
Rita Williams-Garcia	Ron Howard	Rudy Giuliani
Sally Field	Selena	Shirley Temple
Usher		

Library of Congress Cataloging-in-Publication Data
Overbey, Theresa, 1957-
       Michael Jackson / Theresa Overbey.
         p. cm. — (A blue banner biography)
Includes filmography (p.), bibliographical references (p.), and index.
Contents: Becoming a legend — A child star is born — The mimic — The road to fame — The king of pop.
       ISBN 1-58415-216-8 (lib. bdg.)
       1. Jackson, Michael, 1958 — Juvenile literature. 2. Rock musicians — United States — Biography — Juvenile literature. [1. Jackson, Michael, 1958 — Childhood and youth. 2. Entertainers. 3. African Americans — Biography.] I. Title. II. Series.

ML3930.J25O94 2003
782.42166'092--dc20
                                                2003000679

ABOUT THE AUTHOR: Theresa Overbey is an author who enjoys writing for children. She has written various biographies and reference articles for all age groups. In addition, Theresa has a nursing degree and has written articles for several nursing journals. She and her husband Randy are foster parents and reside in Middletown, Delaware.

PHOTO CREDITS: Cover: Globe Photos; p. 4 Neal Preston/Corbis; p. 9 Neal Preston/Corbis; p. 10 Globe Photos; p. 16 Michael Montfort/Globe Photos; p. 19 Neal Preston/Corbis; p. 22 Tom Zimberoff/Getty Images; p. 25 AP Photo/Ira Mark Gostin; p. 27 AP Photo/Bebeto Matthews; p. 28 AP Photo/Kevork Djansezian

CONTENTS

Michael Jackson performing in the look he made famous: a single white glove and sequined jacket. Here, he agreed to sing with The Jacksons one last time during the 1984 Victory Tour.

Becoming a
Legend

*T*he year was 1984. Excitement was in the air as the music industry prepared for its biggest night of the year. All of the celebrities that represented the glamour and glitz of Hollywood were present at the Grammy Awards. A young man sat in the front row wearing a sequined jacket, dark glasses, and a single white glove on his right hand. Sitting next to him were his friends, actress Brooke Shields and Emmanuel Lewis, the pint-sized star of the TV show *Webster*. It was an evening that would be remembered forever because the shy, young man was about to make music history.

The Grammys were special that night. For the first time ever a male performer and his records had been nominated for 12 awards. The man in the front row was on the brink of superstardom. He was about to become one of the most famous singers in the world. His face would be recognized by fans in every country. Just 26 years old, Michael Jackson became the first person to win eight Grammy awards. Mickey Rooney, one of the award presenters that night, told the audience, "It was a pleasure doing the Michael Jackson Show."

Seven of those eight Grammys were awarded to Michael's album *Thriller*. His talent as a singer and songwriter had been well-known to many, but that night Michael, together with Quincy Jones, won the "Producer of the Year" award for *Thriller*. Michael proved to be a man of many talents. He won an award for "Best Children's Album" for *E.T.: The Extra-Terrestrial*.

Many people believe that Michael's childhood was stolen from him because he became a performer at a very young age.

In fact, the special effects of Michael's album *Thriller* and the children's fantasy of *E.T.*, probably best represent who Michael Jackson really is. He has often been considered a little boy in a man's body. He loves the world of make believe. His home in Encino, California is a reflection of a boy who never grew up. Many people believe that Michael's childhood was stolen from him by fame and success, because he became a performer at a very young age. He named his home "Neverland," from the story *Peter Pan*. It represents the world of fantasy because Neverland is every child's dream. On the property there is a zoo with a llama named Louis and a boa constrictor named Muscles. Michael's home has a popcorn machine, and an old-fashioned ice cream and soda fountain. One room in the mansion contains a re-creation of the Pirates of the Caribbean, a popular amusement ride at Disneyland.

Michael was five years old when he joined his family's band, the Jackson 5. He admits not remembering much of those first years of his childhood. What Michael does remember is the music and the work. "I remember singing at the top of my voice and dancing with real joy and working too hard for a child," he once remarked to a reporter.

> **Michael was five years old when he joined his family's band, the Jackson 5.**

A Child Star is Born

Michael Joseph Jackson was born on August 29, 1958. He was the seventh of nine children born to Joe and Katherine Jackson. They lived in a tiny three room home at 825 Jackson Street in the industrial city of Gary, Indiana. From the beginning, even when Michael was a baby, his mother noticed something different about him. "You know how babies move uncoordinated, Michael was never that way," she recalled.

Joe Jackson grew up in a strict household where he learned that survival in the world meant hard work. He had musical talents and played guitar for a band called the Falcons. Katherine was a strict Jehovah's Witness and her faith influenced the way she raised her children. She also loved music and played both the clarinet and the piano.

Maureen, Joe and Katherine's first child, was born in 1950. She was followed by Jackie, Tito, Jermaine, La Toya, Marlon, Michael, Randy and Janet. Joe and Katherine believed in strong family values and they tried to instill them in their children. Michael has early childhood memories of two loving parents.

Both of Michael's parents were concerned about raising a family in Gary, Indiana. It was a rough suburb of Chicago, and Katherine feared that her boys would become involved in gangs. She worked hard at keeping her family home and together. She organized card and

Several members of the Jackson family relax outside their home. Michael is seated, first on the left.

A young Michael Jackson daydreaming about his future. Michael's father, Joe Jackson, gave up his dreams of becoming a rock star in order to support his large family.

board games as entertainment. Often, the children watched their father's band practice in the living room of their home. Eventually Joe Jackson, who worked as a crane operator in a steel mill, had to give up his dreams of being a rock musician to support his family.

The Jackson family often gathered in the living room and made its own music. Joe played the electric guitar. Katherine sang and played the piano. They noticed that all of their children sang well and seemed musically gifted. Joe enjoyed the musical time with his family, but he warned the children not to touch his prized possession, the electric guitar. "The closet where the guitar was kept was considered sacred," Michael recalled.

Tito, the bravest of the bunch, decided to see if he could play the guitar. He took it from the closet and brought it into the bedroom. Tito, Jackie, and Jermaine would play while four-year-old Michael watched. One day, the brothers broke one of the strings on their father's guitar. They panicked and returned the guitar to the closet. Joe was very angry when he learned that his sons had been in the closet, used his guitar, and broken a string.

He went to Tito's bedroom carrying the guitar with the broken string and demanded to know what had happened. Tito admitted that he was the one that broke the string. Joe insisted that Tito play the guitar for him. Tito was afraid of his father's anger, but once he started playing his father calmed down. Joe realized that his son had talent. He listened to his other sons play and decided that he had enough talent in his own family to start a band.

> *Tito, the bravest of the brothers, took their father's guitar from the closet to see if he could play it.*

CHAPTER 3

The Mimic

*J*oe bought second-hand instruments for his older children. Tito and Jackie played the guitar. Jermaine played the bass guitar. Maureen and La Toya accompanied on violin and clarinet. The boys took turns singing. Since Michael was only four, his parents felt that he was too young to be in the band. The younger children were the band's first audience. Michael loved watching his older brothers and sisters. Eventually, Maureen and La Toya got tired of all the practicing and they dropped out. The group became an all-boy band.

Joe loved the idea of his sons being in a band, but Katherine had mixed feelings about it. She was concerned about the money spent on instruments and the amount of time the children practiced. She did, however, like the idea of the family being together so she went along with her husband's wishes.

Joe was determined to make his children successful. He made sure they practiced every day after school. When Michael was five years old his father decided to include him in the band. He had noticed Michael watching his brothers and mimicking Jermaine singing lead while playing the bongo drums at the same time. Almost immediately, Michael took over as the group's lead singer. None of his brothers minded. "Michael was so energetic that at five years old he was like a leader and we saw that," Jackie remembers.

They discovered that Michael was a talented mimic. The band used his gifts in their early performances. They based much of their show on imitating the moves of other popular groups. Michael copied many of the dance moves of the early Motown artists. Sam Cooke and James Brown were two of Michael's favorite performers. He later recalled, "I was like a sponge watching everyone and trying to learn everything I could."

Michael's father was determined to make his children successful. He made sure they practiced every day after school.

Joe Jackson and his family practiced for three years before he felt they were ready to show their talents. He wanted his band to be very professional. Michael remembers entering the first grade in 1964 and rushing home after school to practice until dinner. Once the meal was over, the boys would practice again. "We always rehearsed," Michael recalled. "Sometimes late at night we'd have time to play games or play with toys, we'd have time to play a game of hide and seek or we'd jump rope, but that was about it. The majority of our time was spent working. I clearly remember running into the house with my brothers when my father came home, because we'd be in big trouble if we weren't ready to start rehearsals on time."

Michael's first solo performance was in the first grade. He received a great ovation from his fellow classmates when he sang "Climb Every Mountain" from *The Sound of Music* in a school program. It was the first time he had experienced a response from a live audience. He realized he loved making people happy with his singing.

> **Michael's first solo performance was in a school program in the first grade.**

CHAPTER 4

The Road to Fame

*I*n 1965 Joe Jackson decided that his family was ready. He entered the boys in local talent shows. Michael was seven years old when they performed at Roosevelt High School in Gary. Katherine made matching vests for them to wear at their first real performance. The group sang and danced to "My Girl," a Temptations hit song. The Jackson family won first prize in that contest. They went on to win top prizes against stiff competition in two other local talent shows.

Their first paid show was for a nightclub called Mr. Lucky's. The Jackson 5 played five shows each night, six days a week. They made between $5 and $8 a night plus whatever money people tossed up on the stage. Michael invented dance steps, and picking up the money became part of his dance routine. "I remember

Michael and The Jackson 5 demonstrating dance moves inspired by Motown artists Sam Cooke and James Brown.

my pockets being so full of money I couldn't keep my pants up," he said.

Once the group started making money, Joe Jackson quit his job at the steel mill to manage the band full time. The entire family spent their weekends in a borrowed Volkswagen Minibus traveling to neighboring states to perform. The money the boys made was used to support the family since Joe was no longer bringing home a paycheck. The family would arrive home early each Monday morning and the children were expected to wake up and make it to school on time.

This schedule was hard on all the kids, but it was especially difficult for Michael. He had become a shy boy and did not make friends easily. He felt most comfortable on stage performing. He used his allowance to pay the kids in the neighborhood to be friends with him. Michael missed out on a lot of normal childhood stuff, but he had many experiences other kids never imagined. He watched live performances of his idols James Brown and Jackie Wilson. He spent a lot of time backstage watching them dance and memorizing their steps.

Michael was a shy boy and did not make friends easily. He felt most comfortable on stage.

In 1967 the Jackson 5 recorded their first single with a local record company called Steeltown. Michael sang the lead for "I'm a Big Boy Now." It was a hit locally, but it never became a well-known song.

The Jackson 5's big break came when they had the opportunity to sing at the famous Apollo Theatre in Harlem, New York. Michael was ten years old in 1968 when they gave their first performance. That special night the boys won the talent show and received a standing ovation. After that, Michael and the Jackson 5 were asked to come back and give a paid performance.

Gladys Knight and the Pips performed regularly at the Apollo. Gladys met the Jackson 5 and heard them sing. She thought they were great and recommended them to her record label, Motown. At about the same time, Diana Ross met the boys. She was dating Berry Gordy, the president of Motown Records. She wanted him to meet the Jackson 5. Two months after performing for Gordy in his home, the Jackson 5 landed a recording contract with Motown.

The Motown contract changed the lives of Michael and his family. In 1969 the boys moved to California, and released their first hit single. They also appeared on national television on the *Ed Sullivan Show*.

> **The more popular the Jackson 5 became, the less privacy the family had.**

Their first hit single was "I Want You Back," and Michael sang the lead. It rose to number one and sold two million copies in six weeks. "ABC," their next single, sold two million copies in three weeks. "ABC" later won the group its first Grammy award. Michael was pleased with their success. He felt that all the hard work was paying off, but there was a price to pay.

The more popular they became, the less privacy the family had. By 1971 the Jackson family was living in a six-bedroom home in Encino, California. The boys were not able to attend public school because of their popularity, so they went to the Walton School, a small pri-

Michael Jackson doing what he loved best: performing with the Jackson 5 for a television audience.

vate school in Los Angeles. When they were on tour, they were taught their lessons by a private tutor hired by Motown. It was difficult for them to go anywhere without being mobbed by fans. Michael was affected by the fanfare the most. Perhaps it was because he was the youngest in the band. Before he started regularly performing in public he had been an outgoing, energetic kid. As the Jackson 5's fame increased, he became shy and quiet. He said once, "Being mobbed hurts. You feel like you are spaghetti among thousands of hands. They're just ripping and pulling your hair. And you feel at any moment you are just going to break." Even though being famous was difficult, Michael and the rest of his brothers were proud of the example they were setting for others. Their success became a source of pride for other black chilren and teens.

> *Even though being famous was difficult, Michael and his brothers were proud of the example they were setting for others.*

The King of Pop

Michael became the first Jackson brother to record his own single. "Got to Be There" was an immediate success and quickly rose to number one on the record charts. His first record sold one million copies. This was the beginning of Michael's solo career, although he still recorded albums with the Jackson 5. In 1972 he recorded his first solo album, *Ben*. Michael loved animals, so "Ben" was one of his favorite songs. It was about a little boy whose best friend is a rat. "Ben" won Michael another gold record award.

As Michael's solo career took off, more changes began to take place for the Jackson 5. They decided to leave Motown Records so that their group could better control the music they wrote and sang. In 1976 Michael and his family signed with Epic Records. The group struggled in the beginning with the new label, but

Michael (front right) in his first acting role. In 1978 he played the part of the Scarecrow in the movie The Wiz. *He co-starred with Diana Ross as Dorothy, Nipsey Russell (back right) who played the Tin Man, and Ted Ross (left) who was the Cowardly Lion.*

Michael's solo career soared. He became more involved in learning all the aspects of the music industry. Michael even became an actor in 1978. He starred with his friend Diana Ross in the movie *The Wiz*. It was based on the story line from *The Wizard of Oz*. Michael discovered that he loved to act. *The Wiz* was never a big box office hit, but it influenced the rest of Michael's career.

When Michael was 21, he decided to break away from the family and go out on his own. He did not sign another contract with his father. He wanted to be his own manager. Joe was angry over this, but Michael felt it was the best decision for his future. When asked about it, Michael replied, "I did not like the way certain things were handled. Mixing family and business can be a delicate situation. All I wanted was control over my own life. And I took it." Michael was truly on his own.

Unlike a lot of other stars, Michael controlled every aspect of his career. He knew how much money he earned from the sale of all his records in the United States and other countries around the world. He was involved in every part of his career and actively managed his lawyers and accountants.

Michael was involved in nearly every part of his career and actively managed his lawyers and accountants.

Michael believed that he was ready to produce his first album. While making *The Wiz,* he met music producer Quincy Jones. Quincy offered to help Michael produce his next album *Off the Wall.* Michael's fans loved the album and it sold nearly six million copies in the United States. Michael was disappointed that the album only received one Grammy nomination that year. He vowed that his next album would really be noticed. He dreamed about creating an album that would be the best selling album of all time.

Quincy and Michael partnered again on his next album, *Thriller,* which was released in 1982. At the age of 24, Michael Jackson's dream came true. *Thriller* became the biggest selling album in the history of the recording industry. It contained three of Michael's biggest hits: "Beat It," "Billie Jean," and "Thriller." Michael also produced three music videos for this album. His videos were much different from some of the others on TV because they contained a story line. He created a new art form and revolutionized the video industry. Michael's popular songs and exciting dance moves such as the Moonwalk caused critics to nickname him the "King of Pop."

> **Michael's videos were much different from some of the others on TV because they contained a story line.**

The 1980s were successful years for Michael. After *Thriller* he collaborated again with his family and produced an album called *Victory.* Even though Michael was tired of being on the road he agreed to tour with his family once again as the Jacksons for the Victory Tour. After the tour was over he got involved in a project with Disney Studios. He helped design a new ride called Captain Eo for Disney's Magic Kingdom. Michael loved the concept of this ride because it was a film about transforma-

tion and how music can help change the world. Michael believed that his music could change the world.

In 1985 Michael became involved in a project that was very close to his heart. He was deeply disturbed by images on the news of starving people in Africa. The photos of suffering children really upset him. With the help of Quincy Jones, Michael and fellow performer Lionel Ritchie wrote the song "We Are the World." They sang and recorded the song with a star-studded list of performers. A video was released and it raised millions of dollars for the hunger relief effort in Africa. In 1986 "We Are the World" won a Grammy for Song of the Year.

Michael's incredible gifts and musical talents continued to be recognized by his fans and the entertainment industry. He had immense success, wealth and fame, yet he was a lonely individual. The shyness he had experienced as a child only increased as he got older. He felt isolated by his fame.

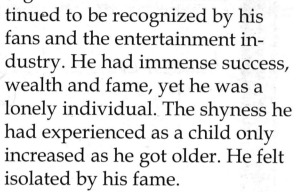

The shyness Michael had experienced as a child only increased as he got older. He felt isolated by his fame.

After his parents divorced in 1982, Katherine Jackson came to live with him in his Encino home. Michael was upset about the divorce, but he had always felt very close to his mother.

Once, when he was asked if he was happy, he replied, "I do not think I am ever happy; what I love is performing and creating. I really do not care about all the material trappings. I love to put my soul into something and have people accept it and like it. That's a wonderful feeling."

As the 1980s brought big changes for his career, the 1990s were a time of personal growth for Michael. He expanded his charitable work, and started the Heal the World Foundation. This charity raises and distributes

Michael Jackson and his first wife Lisa Marie Presley appearing in public at the MTV Video Music Awards in 1994.

funds to causes that aid needy children worldwide. In the summer of 1992 his musical career enabled him to tour the world and visit 15 countries to raise money for the foundation. The successful show was called the Dangerous Tour. Money from his *Dangerous* album was given to the foundation.

Personal problems seem to follow the adult Michael. There were allegations made about Michael concerning misconduct against children. These charges were never proven to be true, but they marred his personal and professional life. He married Lisa Marie Presley in 1994, only to have the marriage end in divorce two years later. He then met Deborah Rowe, a nurse at his dermatologist's office and they married.

Michael seemed to put an end to some of his personal isolation when Deborah had their first child, Prince Michael Jackson in 1997. Their second child, Paris Michael Katherine, was born the following year. Unfortunately, the relationship between Michael and Deborah did not work out and they divorced in 1999. Michael's third child, a son named Prince Michael II was born in 2002. Michael has not revealed the identity of the mother.

No one knows what the future will hold for Michael Jackson, the mature man. His creative genius has motivated and entertained his fans for nearly four decades. Michael Jackson is a legend in his own time. The world will be truly blessed if Michael continues to entertain his fans with his musical gifts. Hopefully, in the future, the legend will continue.

Michael Jackson, the critically acclaimed "King of Pop" performing his hit song "Dangerous" during the taping of a television special.

CHRONOLOGY

1958	born August 29 in Gary, Indiana to Joseph and Katherine Jackson
1963	joins the family band
1964	gives his first public performance to his class
1966	Jackson 5 wins talent show at Roosevelt High School
1968	the Jackson 5 appears at the Apollo Theater in Harlem, New York and signs contract with Motown Records
1969	the boys move to California; "I Want You Back," the Jackson 5's first single with Motown, goes to number one; the Jackson 5's first album, *Diana Ross Presents the Jackson 5,* is released
1970	"ABC" is released and goes to number one
1971	the entire Jackson family moves to Encino, California
1972	Michael's hit "Got To Be There" is released; *Ben,* Michael's first solo album, is released
1976	the Jackson 5 leaves Motown and signs with Epic Records
1979	leaves the Jackson 5 and produces *Off The Wall* with Quincy Jones; wins the role of the Scarecrow in *The Wiz*
1982	*Thriller* is released and eventually sells 50 million copies
1984	wins eight Grammy Awards; joins his brothers for the Victory Tour
1985	"We Are the World" is recorded and released
1991	*Dangerous* is released
1992	starts the Heal the World Foundation
1994	marries Lisa Marie Presley
1996	divorces Lisa Marie and marries Deborah Rowe
1997	son Prince Michael is born
1998	daughter Paris Michael Katherine is born
1999	divorces Deborah Rowe
2001	inducted in to the Rock & Roll Hall of Fame
2002	son Prince Michael II is born

DISCOGRAPHY

With the Jackson 5:

1969   *Diana Ross Presents the Jackson 5*
1970   *ABC*
1970   *Christmas Album*
1971   *Third Album*
1971   *Maybe Tomorrow*
1971   *Goin' Back to Indiana*
1972   *Lookin' through the Windows*
1973   *Skywriter*
1973   *Get It Together*
1974   *Dancing Machine*
1975   *Moving Violation*
1976   *Joyful Jukebox Music*

With the Jacksons:

1976   *The Jacksons*
1977   *Goin' Places*
1978   *Destiny*
1980   *Triumph*
1984   *Victory*

Solo Career:

1972   *Got To Be There*
1972   *Ben*
1973   *Music and Me*
1975   *Forever Michael*
1979   *Off The Wall*
1982   *Thriller*
1987   *Bad*
1991   *Dangerous*
1995   *HIStory; Past, Present, and Future*
1997   *Blood on the Dance Floor*
2001   *Invincible*

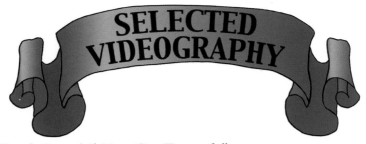

SELECTED VIDEOGRAPHY

1979 "Don't Stop 'til You Get Enough"
1983 "Beat It"
1983 "Billie Jean"
1983 "Thriller"
1987 "Bad"
1988 "Man in the Mirror"
1989 "Leave Me Alone"
1992 "Heal the World"
1995 "Scream"
1996 "They Don't Care about Us"
1997 "Blood on the Dance Floor"

SELECTED AWARDS

1971 Grammy Award for Best Pop Song "ABC"
1980 American Music Award for Favorite Male Soul Artist
1983 Thirteen Billboard Music Award including Best Performance by a Male Artist
1983 Rolling Stone Readers' Poll #1 Artist of the Year
1984 Eight Grammy Awards including Best Album for *Thriller*
1984 Three MTV Video Music Awards including Best Overall Performance "Thriller"
1993 Grammy Award: Living Legend Award
2002 American Music Award for Artist of the Century

FOR FURTHER READING

Graves, Karen Marie. *Michael Jackson.* San Diego: Lucent Books, 2001.

Wallner, Rosemary. *Michael Jackson: Music's Living Legend.* Minneapolis: Abdo & Daughters, 1991.

INDEX